THE BIRMINGHAM TO DERBY LINE

JOHN JACKSON

AMBERLEY

First published 2025

Amberley Publishing
The Hill, Stroud
Gloucestershire, GL5 4EP

www.amberley-books.com

ISBN 978 1 3981 2445 5 (print)
ISBN 978 1 3981 2446 2 (ebook)

British Library Cataloguing in Publication Data.
A catalogue record for this book is available from the British Library.

Origination by Amberley Publishing.
Printed in the UK.

Appointed GPSR EU Representative: Easy Access System Europe Oü, 16879218
Address: Mustamäe tee 50, 10621, Tallinn, Estonia
Contact Details: gpsr.requests@easproject.com, +358 40 500 3575

Contents

Introduction

The background to this publication begins with a seemingly unrelated event that happened back in 1964 and between 50 and 100 miles away to the east. As a youngster brought up in Northampton with family living in East Boldon, between Newcastle and Sunderland, I became used to school holiday rail journeys to visit them. This involved a change of trains, and stations, in Peterborough and a second train change in Newcastle.

Then, on 2 May 1964, the unimaginable happened. The line between Northampton and Peterborough was closed under the so-called 'Beeching Axe'. The railway staff at Northampton's Castle station were quite straight-faced when suggesting to my parents that in future we should travel via London Euston and King's Cross. My parents were flabbergasted at the cost this change of route would involve and resigned themselves to the 'compromise' of a journey around 50 miles westwards instead, with a change of trains in Birmingham's New Street station.

As a result, in July 1965, I was to experience my first travel on the line between Birmingham and Derby. Little did I know at the time that I would be travelling these 40 miles throughout the next sixty years, often several times a week.

During that sixty-year period much has, of course, changed along this key 'cross-country' route through the Midlands. The constant stream of loco-hauled passenger trains, particularly on a summer Saturday, has all but ceased. The regular passing of coal trains along much of the route has also been consigned to history. Then in the mid-1990s along came rail privatisation, perhaps the biggest change of all.

In this publication, we follow the 40-mile route between Birmingham and Derby, exploring the variety of rail traffic seen over the last twenty years or so. Back in 1965, the line still enjoyed steam traction, with the depot at Saltley, near Birmingham city centre, used by steam locomotives for a further year or two until being closed to steam in March 1967, and the depot itself has since been demolished. The depot area remained in use for diesel stabling and maintenance until around the time of the millennium. Whilst I have no photographic archives from those early days of travelling the line, a nostalgic look back at diesel stabling in Saltley's later years is included in this publication.

Our journey commences at Birmingham's much-maligned station at New Street and follows the route through the city's suburbs, including Saltley and the nearby Freightliner container terminal at Lawley Street, and across the county border into Warwickshire, to the village of Water Orton. The station here is a popular venue for rail enthusiasts, although little known to the wider world. It's popularity is due to its location being a busy junction between the line to Derby and an eastward fork towards Coleshill, Nuneaton and Leicester.

Much of Birmingham's freight activity is also centred on the railway network in a triangle of lines formed by this junction at Water Orton (see map on page 7). Two more busy container terminals are located at Hams Hall and Birch Coppice together with a rail-served oil terminal and scrap terminal at Kingsbury.

Crossing into the county of Staffordshire, we also take a detailed look at the traffic found at the line's two most important intermediate stations. These are at Tamworth (High Level) and Burton-on-Trent. The station at Tamworth, in particular, is another popular location for rail enthusiasts with its split-level station located where the Birmingham to Derby line on the High Level crosses at right-angles with the West Coast Main Line at the Low Level below.

Our journey concludes with a selection of photos taken within the Derby area. The city itself has a long association with the railway industry and, despite several near closures, its workshops have survived and they build and maintain a variety of rolling stock there to this day.

This important cross-country route between Birmingham and Derby forms a strategic part of the longer-distance passenger rail network linking Scotland, the North East and Yorkshire with Bristol, South Wales and the West Country.

It is, however, the variety of freight traffic that draws the rail enthusiast to this Midlands area. The frequent passing of coal trains may have ceased, but this key stretch of railway still has a lot to offer. From oil and steel, to aggregates and container traffic, all the country's main freight operators are regular visitors to the area.

I hope you enjoy your journey through the pages that follow as much as I have enjoyed compiling them.

John Jackson

Map of the Area Covered in This Book

Birmingham to Derby Line

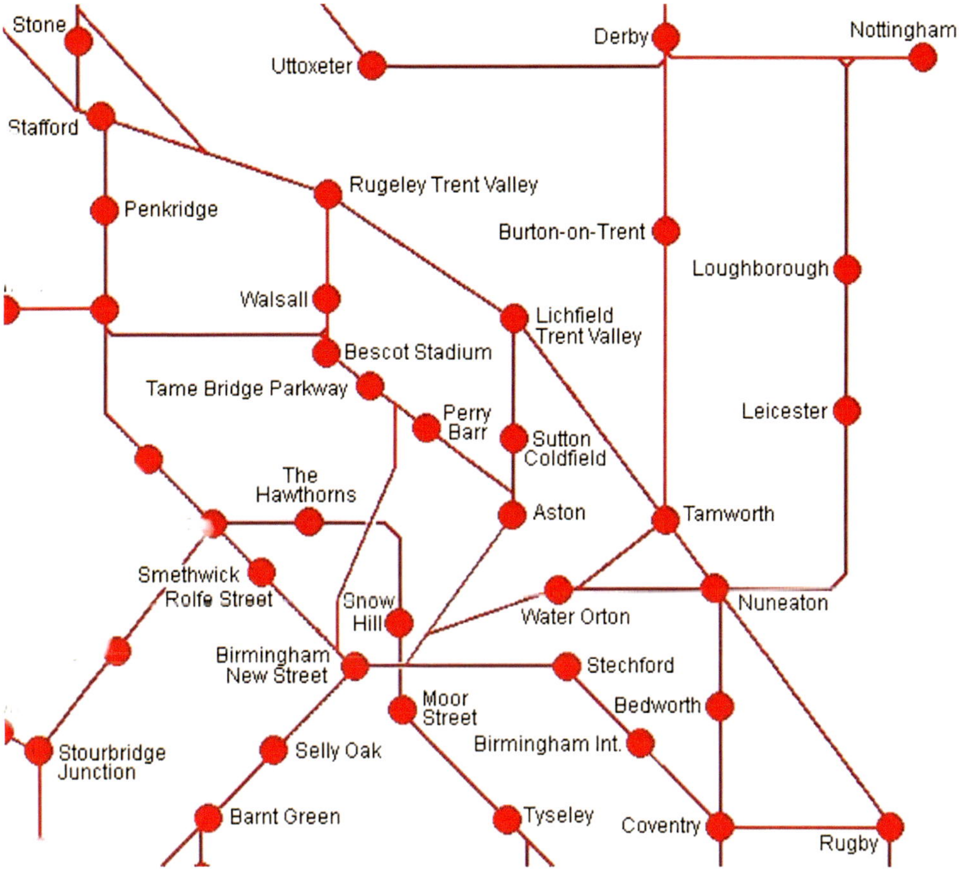

Rail map showing passenger lines around the Birmingham area. The principal stations covered in this publication are Birmingham New Street, Water Orton, Tamworth, Burton-on-Trent and Derby. Some freight-only lines are not shown.

Setting the Scene

In this publication, our 40-mile journey to Derby commences in the heart of Birmingham's city centre. This view shows New Street station's entrance in April 2019.

The underground platforms have offered little natural light, creating a generally grim experience for rail travellers ever since the 'new' station opened in 1967. This 1991 view of Brush Type '4' locomotive 47838 shows the uninviting darkness beyond.

Our journey will take us through Water Orton, Tamworth and Burton-on-Trent. This is an area with an enduring popularity amongst railway enthusiasts. Hopefully, the pages that follow will demonstrate why that is, by showing the railway variety on offer. At Tamworth, roughly the halfway point on this stretch of railway, the Birmingham to Derby line crosses over the West Coast Main Line (WCML). The two High Level platforms are situated on the over bridge in the centre of this view, taken from the London-bound Low Level platform, looking south.

Journey's end is 40 miles away at Derby, a city with a long association with Britain's railway history. This 2014 view shows the city's station entrance.

Birmingham New Street and Its Eastern Approach

The Birmingham New Street to Derby line has a long association with the InterCity 125 (HST), just as it had with the Brush Types, later to become the Class 47s. Carrying an early livery for the class, HST power car 43160 is seen at New Street on 5 May 1990.

Over thirty years later and, of course, within a privatised railway, CrossCountry continued to use the HST sets to supplement its Voyager services. With their days now numbered, power car 43378 stands in New Street on 4 April 2023.

The South Tunnel from New Street heads eastwards and reaches Proof House Junction. On 7 September 2018, power car 43357 passes the junction on its approach to New Street on a service to Plymouth.

Lines diverge at the junction here to Duddeston (Cross-City), Adderley Park (Coventry & WCML), Camp Hill (towards King's Norton) and the Derby line. In a photo taken from the Cross-City Line, CrossCountry unit 170522 approaches the junction from the Derby direction.

A mile or two from New Street, to the left (west) side of the Derby line is the Birmingham Freightliner Terminal (FLT), with a postal address on Landor Street, but referred to in railway terms as Lawley Street. With the giant gantry cranes dwarfing over the yard, this is the view from a passing passenger train in October 2024.

The Lawley Street FLT is served by regular intermodal container trains from Southampton, Felixstowe and London Gateway. The terminal occupies a site of around 35 acres and can accommodate over 4,000 20-foot containers. These numbers may, however, be impacted by the extensive works nearby in connection with HS2.

Saltley Depot

The former depot at Saltley was to the east side of the line, opposite this Freightliner terminal. Although the shed closed to steam in 1967 and the local passenger station shortly after, the site remained a diesel locomotive inspection point until the mid-2000s. In 1991, locos stabled here included Class 20s such as 20110, seen here stabled outside the depot building.

These English Electric Type '1' locomotives were usually stabled here in pairs, with sister loco 20031 stabled alongside 20110 that day. Both these veteran machines survive in preservation. Built back in 1959 as D8131, 20031 is now preserved on the Keighley & Worth Valley Railway, whilst 20110 is at the Embsay & Bolton Abbey Steam Railway.

Saltley was also a stabling point for Brush Type '2' (Class 31) locos in the years running up to privatisation in the mid-1990s. 31424 was in a line of diesels in this view from 1991.

In March the previous year classmate 31423 is seen stabled at Saltley. This InterCity-liveried loco was to be named *Jerome K. Jerome* at the open day at nearby Bescot depot a few months later.

It is seen stabled alongside English Electric Type '3' 37083 that day. These long-serving Class 37 machines remain hugely popular amongst rail enthusiasts. This particular loco was to complete almost forty years' service before being cut up at Immingham depot in 2000.

Another blue-liveried Class 37 loco, 37214, is seen stabled on the depot in April 1990. This diesel entered traffic back in early 1964 and, sixty years later, it survives at the Bo'Ness & Kinneil Railway.

The depot was regularly home to a cluster of Brush Type '4' locomotives. In this view, four different Class 47 liveries are on display. From left to right: 47833, 47051, 47238 and 47459 are present. 47051 carried the unofficial name *Great Snipe*.

With a pair of Class 37s for company, 47286 is seen stabled alongside the depot building in this May 1991 view. This 1966-built loco was to survive until 2000, when scrapped by English, Welsh & Scottish Railway (EWS) at their Springs Branch, Wigan depot.

I was to be a regular weekend visitor around this time, particularly hoping to find several Class 58 locomotives stabled. On this day in 1991, they included 58009, which is sporting the decals of Railfreight's Coal Sector. EWS decided to withdraw the entire class in 2002, and 58009 was to be exported to France, being scrapped at Alizay in 2023.

This was the familiar view on reaching Saltley depot in the 1990s. Sister loco 58011 also sports Railfreight Coal decals in this line-up. Once named *Worksop Depot*, reflecting its area of operation in its British Rail days, this loco was also to be withdrawn in the UK in 2002, after less than twenty years' service. It was scrapped in France in 2023.

By the end of the 1990s, English, Welsh & Scottish Railway (EWS) had superseded British Rail as the users of Saltley, now operating in the privatised era. The company was also in the process of adopting an 'out with the old, in with the new' loco policy when this 1999 photo was taken. On the right, 58030 has just a couple more years left in service, whilst on the left is General Motors' 66053, the new order for EWS in the privatised era.

On 27 January 2017, 66060 stands in the Saltley area. By then, most of the railway buildings had been demolished, but locos were still stabled in the sidings here, notably in between banking duties at the Lickey incline, around 15 miles to the south of here.

Water Orton

Just over 7 miles from Birmingham New Street lies the Warwickshire village station at Water Orton. The unstaffed station offers an uninviting entrance from the road bridge above the railway, with no facilities other than a small 'bus stop'-style waiting area.

At platform level, the three tracks through here are split by an island platform, allowing the limited number of daily services to make the call here. The left-hand platform is used for just one northbound departure to Derby each weekday. The right-hand platform is marginally busier, with a handful of the services between Birmingham and Leicester calling here in both directions.

These services are operated by CrossCountry (XC) with one of their two-car units, 170522, calling on 5 June 2014 on a Leicester to Birmingham service.

Almost all of CrossCountry's services pass without calling at Water Orton, including all but one of those services on the route linking Nottingham, Derby, Birmingham, Gloucester and Cardiff Central. On 20 April 2021, three-car unit 170102 approaches on a service from Nottingham. The line towards Coleshill, Nuneaton, Leicester and East Anglia veers off to the right of this view.

The longer-distance CrossCountry services on the north-east to south-west axis are in the hands of the company's fleet of Class 220 and Class 221 Voyager diesel units, often working in pairs. On 24 August 2021, a five- and four-car pairing of 221138 and 220025 approach Water Orton on a southbound service.

Until recently, these Voyagers were complemented by the use of pairs of the much-loved High Speed Train (HST) power cars on their long-distance passenger services. On 11 August 2020, 43304 leads a HST rake on a service heading for Birmingham, and onwards to Bristol and Plymouth.

Water Orton's station platforms and their immediate surrounds are a popular location amongst enthusiasts and photographers, with many freight services using this section of the Derby to Birmingham line, as well as the eastbound route towards Nuneaton. DB Cargo's 66148 *Maritime Intermodal Seven* heads north on an intermodal working from Southampton to Masborough (Rotherham).

In addition to this main Derby to Birmingham line, just to the west of the station there is a freight-only spur which avoids Birmingham city and is used to reach the Bescot and Walsall area, via Sutton Park. Passenger services were gradually reduced with the few remaining into the early 1960s being withdrawn in January 1965. The Royal Mail terminal at Sutton Park remained in use for a further twenty years or so. GB Railfreight's 66735 *Peterborough United* has just emerged from this Sutton Park line and is passing Water Orton on a Bescot to Toton engineers' working.

By twenty-first-century freight volumes, this village station on the fringe of Birmingham is one of the busiest stretches of line in the country. All the major operators operate services through this immediate area, as evidenced on the selection of workings shown on the next few pages. On 1 September 2020, DB Cargo's 66050 heads westwards on returning empty steel wagons from Corby to Margam, South Wales.

A year later, on 24 August, the same working is in the hands of DB Cargo's 66148 *Maritime Intermodal Seven*. This locomotive carries the livery of Maritime Transport Ltd, recognising the intermodal service jointly offered by both companies.

Another regular DB Cargo steel working links the steel terminal at Wolverhampton with the South Humberside port of Immingham. On 20 April 2021, the return working to Immingham was double-headed by the pairing of 66118 and 66011.

By the 2020s only a handful of DB Cargo's Class 60 locos remained in traffic. On 26 April 2022, one of them, 60066, was rostered to work this service, at least as far as the company's sidings at Toton yard.

One of the DB Cargo services that no longer operates saw regular Class 60 locomotive workings between Lindsey Oil Terminal and Westerleigh, near Bristol. On 22 January 2015, 60059 *Swinden Dalesman* heads through Water Orton platform with the northbound working. The Bristol terminal remains rail-served, with trains operating to and from Robeston in South Wales since 2016.

Another working no longer operated by DB Cargo is the regular infrastructure working between Scunthorpe, Doncaster and Eastleigh. This 2015 view shows 66121 passing the station's platform on the southbound working. This working is currently in the hands of GB Railfreight.

Around half the bulk production of cement from the Breedon works at Hope, in Derbyshire, is moved by rail. It is now the largest producer of cement, by tonnage, in the UK. The destinations served include the Breedon terminal at Walsall. In July 2014, DB Cargo's 60100 is heading to Walsall on a loaded working from Hope.

DB Cargo's 66090 *Maritime Intermodal Six*, another of their Maritime-liveried locos, is seen heading in the opposite direction on 20 April 2021. It is returning a rake of empty wagons from Breedon at Walsall. This time, the Derbyshire destination is Dowlow quarry, located on a short spur from Buxton.

The quarries in Leicestershire are also contributors to the volume of freight traffic on this section of the Birmingham to Derby line. On 25 June 2020, 66012 passes under the station overbridge and is about to take the line towards Leicester. The train is a working from Bristol to the quarry sidings at Mountsorrel.

A number of DB Cargo-operated intermodal trains also pass through the junction at Water Orton. Most of these are services to and from the docks at Felixstowe and Southampton. This working, hauled by 66006, is approaching the station on 16 February 2016 on a working from Felixstowe to Burton-on-Trent.

Many of the Freightliner-operated services to and from Lawley Street terminal in Birmingham pass through Water Orton including this lunchtime working to London Gateway. It is seen on 22 September 2022 being hauled by their Class 66 locomotive 66546.

Heading westbound on 11 August 2020, Freightliner's 66413 *Lest We Forget* is seen sporting the parent company livery of Genessee & Wyoming. It has just left the nearby container distribution terminal at Birch Coppice and is returning to Felixstowe. It will reach the Suffolk port via the Sutton Park line, Aston and Stechford before following the West Coast Main Line towards London.

Another Freightliner departure from the nearby terminal at Lawley Street passes through on 1 June 2021, with 70019 in charge. The Class 70 is heading to Southampton via Nuneaton and the West Coast Main Line.

Another Class 70 duty on 1 October 2013 saw 70004 *The Coal Industry Society* pass Water Orton on an infrastructure working from Crewe to Toton.

The demise of railborne coal traffic had a considerably detrimental effect on the overall volume of freight traffic on the Birmingham to Derby line. Rugeley Power Station, in Staffordshire, used to receive regular coal deliveries from both North and South Humberside, routed through Water Orton. On 1 September 2015, 66615 passes the station platform on a loaded working of imported coal from Immingham Docks to Rugeley.

In February 2016, another loco from Freightliner's Heavy Haul Class 66/6 sub class, 66616, is seen on an empty coal hopper working, returning from Rugeley. The destination is the holding sidings at Barnetby, prior to the rake later returning to Immingham, South Humberside, for further loading.

With the loss of coal traffic, Freightliner's Heavy Haul Sector has relied more heavily on aggregates traffic. Many of these workings utilise the lines in the Water Orton area. On 1 June 2021, 66604 heads west with a rake of hoppers from Radlett, on the southern end of the Midland Main Line, to East Usk Yard, Newport.

On 11 August 2020, 66592 *Johnson Stevens Agencies* heads in the opposite direction with its rake of empty aggregate hoppers. They are returning from Banbury to the substantial quarry at Tunstead, in Derbyshire.

On 20 May 2014, 66616 passes the station platform on a working from Bardon Hill quarry, in Leicestershire, to Willesden. This train will take the circuitous route via Sutton Park, Aston and Stechford, before reaching North London via the West Coast Main Line.

Freightliner operates a number of freight services daily to and from Earles Sidings, at Hope Cement Works in Derbyshire. These include workings to and from Breedon at Walsall. Often bringing a Class 70 locomotive to the area, it is the turn of 70017 on 1 June 2021.

A few weeks earlier, on 20 April, it was rumoured, but not confirmed, that the allocated loco for this working, 70008, was in trouble en route. What is known is that 66420 was added at Toton and the pair resulted in a double-header as they approached Water Orton. This working is particularly popular amongst wagon enthusiasts as it brings the short wheelbase 'PCA' tanks to the area.

Direct Rail Services (DRS) have a long-established contract for intermodal movements on behalf of their customer Tesco. These workings from Daventry International Rail Freight Terminal (DIRFT) include a daily working to and from the rail terminal at Wentloog, in Cardiff. On 22 September 2020, it's the turn of 66303 to appear on the Wales-bound loaded service.

A more recent addition to these services is this working from DIRFT to Doncaster. On 24 August 2021, 66427 is seen passing through the station on its outbound journey to Doncaster. It will take the curve towards Kingsbury on reaching Whitacre Junction.

In addition to these intermodal duties, DRS also handle some infrastructure work on behalf of Network Rail. This frequently brings their Class 68 locomotives to Water Orton. On 8 December 2015, 68017 *Hornet* appears out of the gloom and approaches the platform end on a Crewe to Toton working, which operates via Bescot Yard.

Having been displaced from their duties with TransPennine Express (TPE), the locos from this TPE pool now make occasional appearances on this working. On 21 July 2020, 68023 *Achilles* heads towards Toton with a short rake of empty wagons.

A decade ago, a similar working produced a much more unusual choice of locomotive. On 22 July 2014, a pair of DRS veteran Class 57s was chosen. With 57008 tucked in behind, 57009 passes the station platform and heads for Toton Yard.

An increasing number of GB Railfreight (GBRf) services operate in the Water Orton area. Unlike the other major players, GBRf was launched after the privatisation of the railways in the mid-1990s and has steadily gained market share ever since. One of their more recent business gains is the service between Scunthorpe, Doncaster and Eastleigh. This southbound working on 1 September 2020 consisted of a light engine move by 66718 *Sir Peter Hendy CBE*.

Heading in the opposite direction on 25 June 2020 is classmate 66720, on another working from Eastleigh Yard, near Southampton. This time the rake of empty ballast box wagons is being tripped to the Leicestershire quarry of Mountsorrel for loading.

One of GBRf's original batch of seven Class 66 locomotives, 66704 *Colchester Power Signalbox*, is seen approaching Water Orton on 7 July 2020. It is returning from another Leicestershire quarry, at Stud Farm, Bardon Hill, with a loaded rake of aggregates heading back to Bescot Yard.

On the same day, appropriately named 66747 *Made in Sheffield* is passing Water Orton on a working from Tinsley, Sheffield. It is tripping its rake of hopper wagons to Coton Hill, near Shrewsbury.

On 20 April 2021, 66729 Derby County passes Water Orton station on another infrastructure working linking the Network Rail yards at Bescot and Toton. On this occasion, the train consisted of bogie switch and crossing carrying 'IFA' wagons. They will be worked onward from Toton to the nearby yard at Beeston, Nottinghamshire.

The quintet of major freight operators is completed by Colas Rail, with their infrastructure service linking Westbury and Bescot yards probably its most popular working amongst local rail enthusiasts. Colas took over this working about ten years ago and usually provides a Class 70 loco for the train. On this day in 2020, 70802 was in charge.

This working often appears as a light engine move, as on 4 August 2020. That day, 70817 is seen approaching Water Orton with DB Cargo's 66015 for company.

Occasionally, Class 70s are substituted on this Westbury to Bescot working, as on 7 January 2014. One of Colas' small fleet of five Class 66/8s, 66847, was in charge passing Water Orton station with a rake of 'salmon' wagons.

Prior to relocating to Nottingham Eastcroft depot, Colas had loco stabling and servicing facilities at Washwood Heath. This frequently necessitated light engine moves to and from that site. On 20 April 2017, their recently repainted Class 37 locomotive 37254 *Cardiff Canton* is working light engine from Washwood Heath to Derby.

Another Colas light engine move from Bescot Yard occurred on 26 April 2022. A pair of Colas' Class 56 locomotives, with 56090 leading 56049 *Robin of Templecombe 1938-2013*, is seen heading for Doncaster.

The wide variety of light engine moves through this Warwickshire village is evidenced in these next few photos. On 1 June 2021, 37418 *An Comunn Gaidhealach* heads through Water Orton on a Cardiff Canton to Derby move.

Another pair of heritage locos made an appearance on 18 May 2021. With both locos dating back to the late 1960s when new, 20205 and 20227 are seen working from King's Norton to Derby.

On 13 September 2012, Brush Type '2' diesel locomotive 31465 passes through the platform. This loco entered traffic back in 1960 as D5637 and ended its service in distinctive Network Rail yellow livery. At the time of writing, the loco is preserved at the Weardale Railway.

These two Class 73 electro-diesel locomotives date back to 1966 and remain in service with GBRf. Their appearances include use on Network Rail Test Trains, based at Derby, frequently operating to the former Southern Region. On 7 July 2020, 73965 and 73961 *Alison* are heading south on a Derby to Eastleigh working.

A pair of East Midlands Trains' HST power cars are seen working 'back-to-back' as they approach Water Orton on 22 September 2020. The pair are working from their depot at Leeds, Neville Hill, to Long Marston.

Some loco moves are random one-offs, and this steam loco move on 26 April 2022 was no exception. Former LMS Stanier Pacific 6233 *Duchess of Sutherland*, together with its support coach, are approaching Water Orton station. The steam engine is on a working from the National Museum in York to Barry Tourist Railway in South Wales. The loco was scheduled to haul a leg of a forthcoming Great Britain Railtour.

Back in 2014, Network Rail Test Trains were regularly hauled by pairs of Class 67 locomotives, operating in top'n'tail mode. On 5 June that year, 67027 leads, with 67025 on the rear, as this test train is returning to its home base at Derby.

Multi Purpose Vehicles (MPVs) are regular visitors to the area, particularly during the autumn leaf fall season. These units operate on behalf of Network Rail as Rail Head Treatment Trains. This MPV pair, DR98910 and DR98960, were operating an out-and-back diagram from their base at King's Norton, south of Birmingham.

Another temporary working through the area occurred around 7 January 2014. For a few days, former first-generation diesel multiple unit numbered as 960014 was used as a route learner on behalf of CrossCountry. This popular 'bubble car' was returning from Nuneaton to Tyseley depot, in Birmingham. It entered traffic back in 1960 as W55022.

Another Tyseley-based unit, 170502, made an appearance on 22 September 2020. It is seen heading north, taking the line towards Derby.

Making a similar move on 25 June 2020 was a Chiltern Railway Class 165 diesel unit. This two-car unit, 165029, was on a working to Burton-on-Trent from Chiltern Railways' depot at Aylesbury.

Leaving Water Orton, the main route to Derby runs directly for around 10 miles in reaching Tamworth via Kingsbury Junction. Meanwhile a short 'dogleg' using a section of the Leicester line reaches Kingsbury Junction via Coleshill Parkway station and then a spur from Whitacre Junction. This station at Coleshill Parkway is around a mile and a half eastward from Water Orton. On 22 October 2013, 70009 passes the platform on an eastbound Freightliner working.

The rebuilt Coleshill Parkway station was reopened in 2007, on the site of the former Coleshill station which had closed back in 1968. It is served by all CrossCountry passenger services between Birmingham, Leicester and East Anglia. On 23 February 2017, their units 170529 and 170517 meet in the station's two platforms.

The important intermodal terminal at Hams Hall lies adjacent to Coleshill Parkway station, whilst the nearby terminal at Birch Coppice lies just off the mainline junction at Kingsbury. The latter location also offers rail access to both Kingsbury Oil Terminal and European Metal Recycling (EMR). On 17 May 2017, DB Cargos 66165 has just arrived at EMR, Kingsbury, on a working from Alexandra Dock Junction, Newport.

Tamworth High Level

Kingsbury's passenger station eventually closed in 1968. A little further north, the two-platform station at Wilnecote, however, remains open. It is located a couple of miles to the south of Tamworth and is served at two-hourly intervals by CrossCountry trains. Tamworth station is about 18 miles from New Street. On 25 January 2023, 170112 calls on a Birmingham to Nottingham, via Derby, service.

This view, taken on 21 February 2021 from the opposite platform, shows 170521 meeting 170110. These units operate a half-hourly CrossCountry service between Nottingham, Derby and Birmingham. Every other unit working is extended from Birmingham southwards to serve Cheltenham Spa, Gloucester and Cardiff Central.

On 26 June 2024, CrossCountry Voyager 220030 calls at Tamworth on a late-running southbound service. Earlier disruption resulted in this unit forming a service to Plymouth having just commenced its journey at Derby.

As already implied, the iconic HSTs have now been withdrawn from their long-standing CrossCountry services. Power car 43321 brings up the rear of this service departing towards Birmingham on 7 June 2016.

The Class 170 diesel multiple units have seen duty on this route for many years, including service in the days of Central Trains. On 3 September 2002, two-car unit 170520 calls on a southbound service.

The route also sees a variety of one-off unit empty stock movements on behalf of various UK passenger operators. On 15 July 2022, for example, a pair of Northern units, 150270 and 150269, were summoned from storage at Worksop for temporary use by Transport for Wales at Cardiff Canton.

A steady stream of freight traffic is scheduled in between the passenger services on this busy section of the route, including heavy trainloads of oil to the nearby terminal at Kingsbury. On 3 June 2019, Class 60 loco 60059 *Swinden Dalesman* heads through the southbound platform with a loaded working from Lindsey, South Humberside, to Kingsbury.

These southbound services are timed to reach the Kingsbury terminal as soon as the northbound empties have departed. On 12 April 2016, classmate 60044 *Dowlow* heads a rake of empties northbound, returning to the Humber refinery on South Humberside.

The Class 60 locomotives have now been displaced on these DB Cargo services, leaving Class 66s in charge. On 18 March 2022, 66047 *Maritime Intermodal Two* heads for Kingsbury on a loaded working from Humber.

The contract to operate this loaded fuel oil from Lindsey to Kingsbury switched from DB Cargo to Colas Rail in July 2022, with their fleet of Class 70/8 locomotives being the preferred traction. On 25 January 2023, this southbound loaded train is in the hands of 70808.

Colas Rail handled a limited number of coal workings in the last few years of railborne coal operations in the UK. On 26 March 2015, 70810 is seen working a rake of hoppers from Ratcliffe Power Station to Gloucester Yard.

Another Colas Rail freight flow saw steel traffic conveyed between Washwood Heath and Boston Docks. On 26 January 2016, 56087 passes Tamworth with a working to the Lincolnshire port.

Until their depot was relocated to Nottingham, Colas Rail light engine movements to and from their Washwood Heath base were commonplace. On 12 January 2016, the pairing of 37175 and 47739 heads to the depot on a move from Derby.

The company was required to vacate their Washwood Heath base in February 2018 prior to its demolition in connection with HS2 work. Their stabling and servicing was relocated to Nottingham Eastcroft depot. After that date, loco moves emanated from Nottingham such as on 15 July 2022. That day, their locomotive duo of 70805 leading 56049 *Robin of Templecombe 1938-2013* is seen heading to Bescot Yard.

Freightliner Heavy Haul coal trains to and from Rugeley were a regular occurrence until that power station's closure. On 23 January 2014, 66508 is seen passing Tamworth's southbound platform on a loaded working from Hull Docks.

The end for Rugeley B Power Station came in June 2016. A year or so earlier, in May 2015, Freightliner's 66622 hauls a rake of empty hoppers returning from Rugeley to York Yard, for stabling.

The Freightliner container service from Felixstowe to East Midlands Gateway reaches its destination via a circuitous route around the West Midlands. That's the reason for such a working to be heading Eastwards through Tamworth High Level. On 15 July 2022, 66503 *The Railway Magazine* was in charge.

For many years the infrastructure workings linking Bescot and Toton yards were in the hands of DB Cargo (formerly EWS). On 1 February 2017, 66027 is in charge of a substantial rake of ballast hoppers and concrete sleepers on the Toton-bound leg that day.

On 21 March 2012, this working was used to convey a couple of returning Class 66 locos from ECR use in France for servicing at Toton depot. ECR Locos 66226 and 66033 were tucked in behind the haulage loco 66141.

By contrast, one of the dwindling number of DB Cargo's active Class 67 locos is seen running from Bescot to Toton on 27 February 2017. The loco, 67005 *Queen's Messenger*, is one of those usually preferred on 'royal' duties.

The infrastructure working between Bescot and Toton moved from DB Cargo to GB Railfreight in 2019. On 15 July 2022, 66771 *Amanda* is in charge of a very short rake, together with DB Cargo's 66014 for company on its journey to Toton.

One of GBRf's regular intermodal workings brings a Class 66 of theirs through the High-Level platforms on a Southampton to Doncaster working. On 8 November 2024, 66739 *Bluebell Railway* is in charge.

GBRf's unique Class 59 locomotive 59003 *Yeoman Highlander* has seen occasional use this far north of its more usual southern base. On 19 January 2017, it has been rostered to haul this rake of hoppers from Tinsley, Sheffield to Coton Hill, near Shrewsbury.

Another pair of GBRf locos is seen approaching the station on 7 June 2016. The duo, with 73962 *Dick Mabbutt* leading and 73965 on the rear, is heading for the former Southern Region on a Derby to Eastleigh move.

Another working that has changed hands is the aggregate service between Peak Forest and Washwood Heath. It is now in the hands of GBRf. On 13 February 2015, DB Cargo's 66018 was in charge when that company was still the operator.

Direct Rail Services' (DRS) locos make regular appearances through Tamworth's High Level platforms. Sometimes, the workings are one-offs, as in the case here where a pair of their Class 37 locomotives are returning a rake of coaching stock to Nemesis Rail at Burton-on-Trent. On 30 March 2017, 37038 leads 37716 on this working.

Network Rail's Inspection Saloon, named *Caroline*, is a more frequent visitor. On this occasion, on 15th May 2015, 37419 is in charge. The Class 37 loco is returning the saloon to Derby from Cardiff Canton.

As mentioned earlier, DRS locos appear on the Birmingham to Derby line working the infrastructure diagram linking Crewe, Bescot and Toton yards. On 12 April 2016, their pioneer Class 68 loco, 68001 *Evolution*, approaches Tamworth's High Level platforms as it heads to Toton.

The following day, an even more modern traction was provided for the same working on 13 April. Sister Vossloh-manufactured 68016 *Fearless* was in charge that day. The newly built loco had been delivered to DRS towards the end of the previous year. The loco may have been new but the age of the wagons in tow more than compensated!

Tamworth's High Level platforms see a wide diversity of one-off appearances which included this Rail Operations Group working on 15 August 2019. With 57305 on the rear and 47815 *Lost Boys 68-88* leading, the pair are working a rake of barrier vehicles in top'n'tail mode. The ensemble is employed on a move from Leicester to Portbury Docks, near Bristol. They are scheduled to collect a newly delivered multiple unit.

On 13 April 2016, it is a working to the Severn Valley Railway (SVR) that produces that day's surprise working through Tamworth High Level. With 56303 providing the power, it has an un-numbered Class 50 loco in InterCity Swallow livery in tow. The loco was, in fact, 50031 *Hood*, delivered new in 1968 as D431. It was being moved from Derby to the SVR at Kidderminster.

In this publication, the focus is on the Birmingham to Derby line through Tamworth's High Level platforms. What attracts the rail enthusiast to this split-level station is the added bonus of having the busy four-track West Coast Main Line below. This is the view looking down at the London platform from the north end of High Level's Derby-bound platform. On 3 June 2015, London Northwestern Railway's 350376 calls on a Crewe to London Euston service.

On the opposite (northbound) Low Level platform, the Birmingham to Derby line runs behind the scaffolded building with the Birmingham direction to the right and the Derby direction to the left. Meanwhile, at Low Level on 8 February 2019, West Coast Rail Company's 33207 *Jim Martin* passes on a Southall to Crewe move.

In order to maximise railway viewing at this busy location, movement between levels becomes paramount, as evidenced in this typically busy view of the Low Level action on 15 July 2022. DRS's 68006 is seen heading south on an empty stock move involving a TransPennine Express coach set. It is seen sandwiched between a northbound Avanti West Coast Pendolino and a southbound intermodal. The busy scene would have been difficult, if not impossible, to view from the High Level platforms.

Burton-on-Trent

About 4 miles to the south of Burton-on-Trent is the Voyager maintenance depot at Central Rivers, also known as Barton-under-Needwood. It was opened back in 2001 by Bombardier Transportation, adjacent to the Birmingham to Derby line. It also offered easy access for empty stock movements to the single-track spur to the West Coast Main Line at Lichfield. An unidentified four-car CrossCountry Voyager is stabled in this view taken in April 2018. Bombardier Transportation has since been acquired by Alstom.

A mile or so north of Alstom's depot is the servicing facility of LH Group Services, now part of Wabtec. The company's site at Barton-under-Needwood specialises in overhaul of diesel engines, and shunting locos in particular. On 4 January 2017, three Class 08 diesel shunters were on view, 08530, 08531 and 08615. A brief glimpse of this yard is possible from passing passenger trains.

The station at Burton-on-Trent consists of an island platform. The station itself is below street level, with access from Borough Road. This is the March 2017 view looking north, with Borough Road running left to right and the station's access from that road in the centre.

Before looking at the traffic seen through the station, it is worth comparing the view above with this one taken seven years later, in June 2024. The area has been completely transformed with much credit due to the local 'Friends of Burton'. It also offers a much more open view of all trains passing the area. Well done to those involved.

On 13 June 2017, Voyager 220021 passes through Burton-on-Trent station's northbound platform on a CrossCountry service to Newcastle.

HST power car 43207 stands in the southbound platform at the rear of a service heading to Plymouth. This restricted view, showing Borough Road above the power car, is taken from the nearby Travelodge. At least one of their rooms offers this limited view of Burton station platforms and passing trains.

This is the view from Borough Road bridge, looking south on 25 April 2019. GBRf's 66722 *Sir Edward Watkin* passes the station platform with the infrastructure working from Bescot to Toton.

On 16 January 2020, another GBRf Class 66 locomotive, pioneer 66701, passes through Burton. It is working the company's intermodal service from Southampton to Doncaster.

Heading in the opposite direction on 5 February 2019, celebrity locomotive 66779 *Evening Star* is working a rake of returning empty hoppers from Tinsley, Sheffield, to Bardon Hill quarry in Leicestershire. On paper, this working is one of the few to work over the little-used freight-only line from Burton to Leicester via Coalville and Bardon. In reality, track conditions and other infrastructure issues often result in the working being diverted from this route.

Back in 2016, the late afternoon infrastructure service linking Toton with Crewe was in the hands of Freightliner. On 23 May that year, 66618 *Railways Illustrated Annual Photographic Awards* is in charge. It will soon reach Wichnor Junction and take the short branch line from there to Lichfield Trent Valley and join the West Coast Main Line to reach Basford Hall Yard in Crewe.

The Earles Sidings to Walsall cement working is seen with a Class 66 locomotive in charge on 6 June 2018. Loco 66503 *The Railway Magazine* is hauling the usual rake of short-wheelbase 'PCA' wagons.

One of the longest-running container services using the Birmingham to Derby line links Leeds Freightliner Terminal with the port of Southampton. It operates via Birmingham, Oxford, Reading and Basingstoke. On 19 March 2018, 66551 passes a cold Burton-on-Trent with traces of snow still lingering.

Freightliner's heavy haul coal wagons have been routine visitors over the years, but this particular working was a one-off. On 8 February 2019, 66572 heads north through Burton-on-Trent with an empty rake from Southampton to Hunslet Yard, in Leeds.

Freightliner Class 70s are also regular visitors to the Burton area, but not on oil tank trains. On 26 July 2024, 70009 heads towards Kingsbury Oil Terminal with a loaded train. It is operating Colas Rail's Lindsey to Kingsbury service. At the time the Freightliner machine was on hire to Colas Rail.

Another loaded rake of oil tanks is seen on 16 April 2013, when DB Cargo's Class 60 locos were the mainstay on these workings. On that day, 60091 heads for Kingsbury from South Humberside.

By 2019, working Class 60 loco numbers were in decline, with only around twenty examples left in traffic with DB Cargo. On 8 February that year, one of them, 60040 *The Territorial Army Centenary*, heads north through Burton-on-Trent with a rake of steel wagons from Wolverhampton Steel Terminal to Boston Docks.

Back in 2013, the second loaded steel working of the day between Margam and Corby was much more likely to be an afternoon 'runner'. On 22 March that year, 66160 is the loco in charge. It was one of the last DB Cargo workings to be banked up the Lickey incline, near Bromsgrove.

On 26 June 2024, DB Cargo's 66124 has just commenced its return journey from Maurice Hill Transport's yard at the north end of the station. It is returning to Acton in West London. It is another working with a reduced distance to travel if the line from Burton to Coalville and Leicester is open for freight traffic. If not, a journey around the West Midlands and then on to the West Coast Main Line is the longer alternative.

The infrastructure working from Bescot to Toton was still operated by DB Cargo when this photo was taken in 2017. On 14 July that year, 66116 is in charge. On this occasion, it was giving a lift to Greater Anglia Class 90 electric locomotive 90001, which was destined for attention at Toton depot.

As already mentioned, by 2019 this working was in the hands of GBRf. On 23 April that year, the move consisted of a light engine convoy, with 66722 *Sir Edward Watkin* in charge. With DB Cargo's old- and new-liveried locos in tow, the trio made a colourful combination, with 66111 nearest the camera and 66055 *Alan Thauvette* in the centre.

On 1 February 2017, DB Cargo's 66005 has just arrived at Burton-on-Trent and recessed its train into the local Maurice Hill Transport Yard. The Class 66 loco is now in the process of running round its intermodal train, before later returning to Felixstowe.

On 18 February 2020, sister DB Cargo loco 66076 has just left the yard and is about to pass Burton-on-Trent station on its southbound journey. The train consists of 'VGA' vans that are used to carry steel from Cardiff Tidal to Burton. The loco is now about to return the empty vans to South Wales.

For many years, Direct Rail Services (DRS) operated a regular infrastructure working between Crewe and Mountsorrel quarry in Leicestershire. Whilst the outbound working from Crewe ran via Nuneaton and Leicester, the return working was routed via Loughborough, Trent and Stenson Junction, to the north of here. On 9 March 2017, the working is entrusted to 66302.

A different type of traction was provided on 23 May 2016, with Chiltern Railways-liveried 68012 in charge. After passing Burton, the train will be routed from Wichnor Junction to Lichfield Trent Valley in order to reach Basford Hall Yard in Crewe.

With the end-of-platform vegetation at its most intrusive, DRS's 66428 *Carlisle Eden Mind* heads south with the company's intermodal working from Tees to Daventry on 18 February 2020. It will reach the Northamptonshire freight terminal via Water Orton, the Sutton Park Line, Stechford, Coventry and Rugby.

On the same day, a pair of DRS Class 37s is seen approaching the platform end working a Network Rail Test Train from Derby. With 37409 bringing up the rear, sister loco 37424 *Avro Vulcan XH558* leads this working destined for Carlisle. Although its official number is 37424, the lead loco carried the number 37558 at the time.

Approaching the opposite end of the station, Colas Rail's 56096 is surrounded by greenery on 13 June 2017. The steel working originated from Washwood Heath, Birmingham, and is bound for Boston Docks.

The veteran Class 20 locomotives were the usual motive power on a contract to move units between either Derby Litchurch Lane workshops or Old Dalby Test Track, near Melton Mowbray, and London Underground Limited (LUL). These units were usually dragged to the LUL depot at West Ruislip often with a layover at Banbury. On 20 March 2013, 30096 and 20107 are seen with another pair, 20901 and 20905, at the opposite end of the LUL stock. This particular stock working was from Old Dalby to West Ruislip.

On Friday 31 March 2017, another DRS heritage machine, 37069, arrives at Burton-on-Trent on a light engine move from Crewe. It was to accompany sister loco 37716 on charter stock work over the forthcoming weekend. This stock would be collected from Nemesis Rail in Burton-on-Trent.

The Nemesis Rail complex, just to the north of Burton-on-Trent, will be explored in more detail in the pages that follow. Meantime, these two photos taken on Friday 14 July 2017 feature another trio of DRS locos. With 57306 *Her Majesty's Railway Inspectorate 175* leading a pair of Class 37 locos, 37602 and 37606, they, too, are heading to the nearby Nemesis Rail complex.

The pair of Class 37s will attach to a rake of charter coaching stock with 57306 on the opposite end. The trio was to work a Huddersfield to Swansea charter the next day, Saturday 1 April 2017.

Just to the north of Burton-on-Trent station is the site of the former British Rail Wagon Works. The extensive yards and sidings here have been the base of Nemesis Rail since around 2007. The variety of locos and stock on site is evident from these two photos taken on 18 March 2018.

These views are looking south towards Burton station. In this second photo, the main Birmingham to Derby running lines can be seen on the left.

A wide variety of locos can be found within this large complex; some are former British Rail examples and others from former industrial use. On 4 January 2017, for example, former English Electric Type '1' loco 20903 is standing in a line that includes both industrial and Class 08 and Class 09 BR diesel shunters.

On 20 February 2017, Sulzer Type '2' loco D5265 was present. This Class 25 loco had previously been at the Great Central Railway.

This photo of 26011 was taken on 5 March 2014. Although a loco that was for ever associated with the Scottish Region, it was built not too far away from Burton, at the Birmingham Railway Carriage and Wagon Company, back in 1959 as D5311. Having arrived from Barrow Hill in the summer of 2011, the loco remains at Nemesis at the time of writing.

On 17 December 2013, Brush Type '4' loco 47703 was photographed in the Nemesis Rail complex. Since being built by Brush in 1967, as D1960, it has had far too many numbers, duties and liveries to document here. Its uses have varied from Edinburgh to Glasgow push/pull passenger duties to working for Fragonset. In fact, it still sports a faded livery of black with red stripe identified with that defunct rail operator.

The range of stock at this Nemesis Rail site necessitates the use of diesel shunters for internal stock movements. On 4 October 2018, for example, Class 08 shunter 08507 is at work shunting a former Greater Anglia-liveried coach.

At the other end of the complex, another veteran shunter, D3236, built in 1955, is seen at work. The loco carried the number 13236 in this view on 14 July 2017. It is moving coach W6310 around the complex.

Northwards to Derby

The station at Willington, 5 miles further north from Burton-on-Trent, lies about halfway between Burton and Derby. It is a two-platform station and is served by passenger trains between Nottingham, Derby and Birmingham on a broadly two-hour frequency. Meanwhile, CrossCountry Voyagers pass without stopping, as in the case of 221123 on a southbound service on 22 June 2018.

A mile or so north of Willington, the Crewe to Derby line via Stoke-on-Trent and Uttoxeter joins the Birmingham to Derby line. Four miles further north, the little-used station at Peartree remains open, served by just eight trains each weekday. East Midlands Railway (EMR) services between Crewe, Derby, Nottingham and Newark call here twice in the morning peak and twice in the evening peak in both directions. On 31 July 2019, single-car Class 153 unit, 153384, makes a call. These units have now been displaced and EMR Class 170 units usually work these services.

Derby

Turning the clock back thirty years, this Derby to Crewe service was in the hands of British Rail, with first-generation diesel multiple units still seeing service. On 24 May 1990, for example, a Tyseley-based two-car unit, T026, occupies the now removed bay platform 5 and is waiting departure for Crewe.

On 30 July 1994, 60016 *Langdale Pikes* heads south through Derby station working the long-standing aggregates service between Peak Forest and Washwood Heath. This is the view looking north towards the station from London Road Rail Bridge. This loco was later to be renumbered to 60500 and named *Rail Magazine*, marking the 500th issue of that publication.

In the 1990s, the decade of rail privatisation, the lines to the east of the station were used extensively for shunting, stabling and passing trains. On 24 May 1990, 37430 *Cwmbran* pauses at Derby with a Network South East-liveried coach in tow.

A year later, a pair of Class 37 locos heads through Derby on a southbound steel working. The pair are 37042 and 37069 *Thornaby TMD*, seen on 25 May 1991. The latter loco was seen earlier in this publication at Burton-on-Trent in DRS livery.

On 4 August 1992, 31102 *Cricklewood*, in Civil Engineer's Department livery, is seen on a rake of similar-liveried wagons as it trundles south through Derby. The loco was to be scrapped in 2007 at EMR at Kingsbury.

This particular photo from Derby taken later in the 1990s was taken a couple of years after privatisation. By then, the fleet of fifty Class 58s had all been transferred into the ownership of English, Welsh and Scottish Railway (EWS). Their retention by EWS was to be short-lived, with all class members being withdrawn between 1999 and 2002. On 17 October 1997, 58004 is seen working a rake of merry-go-round coal hoppers south through the station.

Much has changed since those 1990s days as these two views, separated by almost half a century, demonstrate. The first, taken in September 1971, shows the view looking across from the 'A' end of platform 6. For the record, D2387 and D5119 can be seen in the background.

By contrast, this June 2018 view shows all those through tracks in the above photo now removed and construction of a further platform at Derby well underway.

Just before the freight loops were sacrificed for the new island platform to be added, a Colas Rail pairing of 67027 *Charlotte* and 67023 *Stella* is using one of these lines in order to reverse and head towards Birmingham. This June 2017 view sees the pair operating in top'n'tail mode.

The privatisation years have seen almost all freight traffic routed away from Derby station, with most using the Erewash Valley route via Toton. An exception, seen on 8 July 2016, was the returning empty hoppers from Tinsley, Sheffield, to Bardon Hill quarry in Leicestershire. On this occasion, GB Railfreight's 66761 *Wensleydale Railway Association 25 Years 1990–2015* was in charge.

A particularly rare working occurred on 13 October 2014. A pair of Class 20s, 20311 and 20314, was called upon to collect 59003 from Immingham Docks, South Humberside. The duo was taking the Class 59 loco to Eastleigh Works for attention. The former Foster Yeoman loco had spent the previous seventeen years in Germany. The author was delighted to see it still carrying its *Yeoman Highlander* nameplate.

The same pair of locos was seen at Derby again on 21 September 2017. In company with another pair, 20107 and 20905, the quartet are about to take the barrier vehicles into Derby's Litchurch Lane works to move a London Underground set to Banbury, initially, and then onwards to West Ruislip.

For many years, there were regular DRS light engine moves between their Gresty Bridge depot and Derby, for both Test Train work and visits for store or attention at Barrow Hill, near Chesterfield. On 21 July 2016, a pair of their Class 37s, 37606 and 37612, arrived along with 68005 *Defiant* and 68022 *Resolution*. The two Class 68 locos were dropped off for forthcoming Network Rail use at Derby Research Test Centre.

The pair of Class 37s then continued to Barrow Hill, where it collected a trio of locos for return to Crewe Gresty Bridge. They returned with 20303, 20305 and 37424 sandwiched between them. The quintet has just been signalled away towards North Stafford Junction.

As already mentioned, Derby has a long tradition of railway engineering with its 175th anniversary celebrated in 2014. The workshops here at Litchurch Lane continue to build railway rolling stock, including the Class 710 units for London Overground. On a wintry 18 January 2018, a pair of Class 710 cars is stabled outside the Litchurch Lane workshops.

The Bombardier workshops also built the Class 720 'Aventra' units, as replacements for a large percentage of Greater Anglia's electric multiple unit fleet. On 31 March 2019, a pair of driving cars is stabled awaiting unit assembly.

Over the years, an extensive variety of locos have been stabled in the area adjacent to the Midland Main Line. With Loram's workshops in the background, this view was taken from a unit arriving on the Birmingham to Derby line on 14 July 2017. A pair of Network Rail's distinctive, yellow-liveried Class 97 locos, 97302 and 97303, is on the left, whilst electro-diesel 73138 is on the right. DRS's 37603 leads the line-up of locomotives in the centre.

On 31 March 2017, another DRS Class 37, 37407, is seen whilst undergoing a major rebuild by Loram. It is un-numbered when seen in this view. Built as D6605 as long ago as October 1965, the loco was withdrawn by its then owners, EWS, in the late 1990s before its expensive 'resurrection' for DRS duties. It was to take up passenger duties the following year between NorwIch, Great Yarmouth and Lowestoft. A year after that, 2019, was to see it named *Blackpool Tower*, in recognition of it regularly working on Manchester to Blackpool services twenty years earlier.

Other Railway Titles by the Author

25 Years of the Class 66
50 Not Out
British Freight Trains
Class 68 & Class 88 Locomotives
Class 70 Locomotives
Containers by Rail in the UK
DB Cargo
East Anglian Traction
Exploring Devon and Cornwall
GB Railfreight
Nameplates
Rail Rover – East Midlands Rover
Rail Rover – Freedom of the Severn & Solent
Railways around The Fens
Railways of Bedfordshire
Railways of Derbyshire
Railways of Leicestershire
Scottish Rail Scene in the 21st Century
Second Generation DMU's
Second Generation EMU's
Survivors of Beeching
Trains around Doncaster
Trains around Eastleigh & Southampton
Trains around Peterborough
Trains on the Midland Main Line
Trains through Nuneaton